American Politics Today

The Modern Republican Party

John Ziff

ELDORADO INK

Eldorado Ink
PO Box 100097
Pittsburgh, PA 15233
www.eldoradoink.com

Produced by OTTN Publishing, Stockton, New Jersey

CPSIA compliance information: Batch#MAP2016.
For further information, contact Eldorado Ink at info@eldoradoink.com.

First printing

1 3 5 7 9 8 6 4 2

Library of Congress Cataloging-in-Publication Data

on file at the Library of Congress
    ISBN 978-1-61900-092-6 (hc)
    ISBN 978-1-61900-100-8 (pb)
    ISBN 978-1-61900-108-4 (trade)
    ISBN 978-1-61900-116-9 (ebook)

For information about custom editions, special sales, or premiums,
please contact our special sales department at info@eldoradoink.com.

Table of Contents

Chapter 1

Demographics and Issues

Reince Priebus, the chairman of the Republican National Committee, painted a stark picture. If the Republican Party's candidate failed to win the presidential race the following year, Priebus told a talk-radio host in June 2015, "we don't exist as a national party."

Given that Republicans held solid majorities in the United States Senate and House of Representatives, the chairman's statement might have seemed hyperbolic. But, as Priebus noted, it's difficult to govern without holding the White House. In addition, the Republican-controlled 114th Congress had done little to inspire the confidence of the American people. Gallup Organization surveys conducted through the first nine months of 2015 found that between 75 percent and 83 percent of the public disapproved of the way Congress was handling its job.

More important to Priebus's point, though, was the recent history of presidential races. Going into 2016, Democratic Party presidential candidates had won the popular vote in five of the previous six elec-

Taxation, gun rights, and health care are among the concerns of these demonstrators protesting the policies of the Obama administration. Members of the Republican Party generally place a high priority on low taxes and limited government.

tions, dating back to 1992. If they suffered another loss, Republicans would be hard-pressed to argue that theirs was a national governing party, a party whose policy ideas still appealed to a majority of American voters.

As it's currently constituted, the Republican Party—often referred to by the nickname Grand Old Party, or GOP—faces unfavorable demographic trends. Groups that identify most strongly with the GOP and its philosophy make up a decreasing share of the population. At the same time, groups that have traditionally supported the Democratic Party are growing.

Furthermore, while Americans have a jaundiced view of politics overall, opinion polling indicates that the GOP has generally been held in lower esteem than the rival Democrats for about a decade. A Gallup survey from July 2015 showed just 35 percent of Americans holding a favorable opinion of the Republican Party, compared with 42 percent viewing the Democratic Party favorably. The last year a majority of the public had a positive opinion of the GOP, according to Gallup, was 2005.

THE BASE: WHO TODAY'S REPUBLICANS ARE

Today's GOP is a conservative party. Political scientists have developed various methods for measuring the ideology of lawmakers. One of the most widely used, known as DW-NOMINATE, is based on roll-call votes. It places legislators on a scale of -1.0 (most liberal) to +1.0 (most conservative). Those who score between -0.25 and 0.25 are classified as moderates. Centrist scores range up to 0.5 from zero (in either direction). Legislators whose scores fall below -0.5 or above +0.5 are deemed highly liberal or highly conservative.

DW-NOMINATE data show that the average Republican in Congress has been growing steadily more conservative since the 1970s. On the whole, Democrats in Congress have gotten more liberal over the same period—but by a smaller margin, according to DW-NOMINATE data. Republican legislators' move to the right far outstripped their Democratic counterparts' move to the left.

In 2015 close to nine in ten Republicans in the House of Representatives ranked as highly conservative on the DW-NOMI-

Republicans tend to hold conservative views on social issues, such as gay marriage and abortion. These anti-abortion protesters are outside a Planned Parenthood clinic in Oregon. In late 2015, Planned Parenthood—a nonprofit organization that provides reproductive health services—became an issue in the GOP presidential primary race due to the release of videos that purported to show members of the organization negotiating the sale of fetal tissue. In response, several Republican candidates urged a ban on federal funding for the organization.

NATE scale. About 45 percent of Republicans in the U.S Senate were non-centrist conservatives.

Self-identified conservatives make up the largest bloc of American citizens who are registered Republicans or who are independents but lean toward the GOP. In a Gallup survey conducted in May 2015, more than half (53 percent) of Republicans and Republican leaners said they were conservative on social issues. Thirty-four percent said they were moderate on social issues, and 11 percent identified themselves as socially liberal. On economic issues, 64 percent of respondents described themselves as conservative, 27 percent as moderate, and just 7 percent as liberal.

Older Republicans are the most consistently conservative. They're also the most likely to vote in primary elections, which is one reason the GOP congressional conference is so conservative.

In presidential races, the conservatism of the GOP's most engaged voters can present a dilemma. To win in the primary elections, Republican candidates often have to stake out very conservative positions. In the general election, though, moderate voters may find such positions unpalatable.

In addition, fewer Americans identify with the GOP than with the Democratic Party. In 2015 the nonpartisan Pew Research Center released an in-depth report on party affiliation, based on more than 25,000 interviews the organization had conducted nationwide the previous year. Pew found that 23 percent of American adults identified with the Republican Party, compared with 32 percent who identified with the Democratic Party. Independents formed the largest group, at 39 percent.

It's long been the norm for more Americans to identify with the Democratic Party than with the GOP. In fact, according to Pew there have been only two years since the 1940s that the Democrats didn't enjoy an edge in party identification: 1995, when the GOP had a 31 percent to 30 percent advantage; and 1991, when party identification was even, at 31 percent each for the Republicans and the Democrats.

Yet Republicans managed to hold their own in presidential elections between 1940 and 2012, winning 9 times to the Democrats' 10. Obviously, party identification isn't determinative in presidential races. The qualities of the specific candidates who are running and the overall environment in which a campaign takes place (for example, the state of the economy, military conflicts, how the public feels about the party in power) matter more.

Nonetheless, the Republican Party faces a demographic challenge that is becoming increasingly serious. "It's an undeniable empirical truth," noted the political analyst Pete Wehner, who served in three Republican presidential administrations, "that the GOP coalition is shrinking."

The Republican Party retains solid support among white voters.

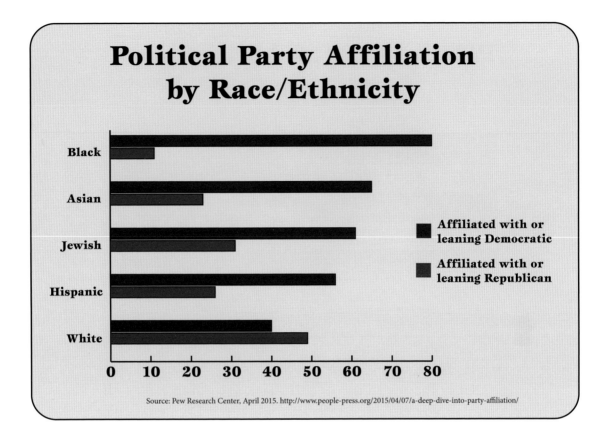

Political Party Affiliation by Race/Ethnicity

Black
Asian
Jewish
Hispanic
White

Affiliated with or leaning Democratic

Affiliated with or leaning Republican

0 10 20 30 40 50 60 70 80

Source: Pew Research Center, April 2015. http://www.people-press.org/2015/04/07/a-deep-dive-into-party-affiliation/

According to the Pew Research Center's 2015 report on party affiliation, 49 percent of white Americans identify with or lean toward the GOP, compared with 40 percent who identify with or lean toward the Democratic Party. The overall Republican advantage among whites is driven by huge margins within certain subgroups. White evangelical Protestants align with the GOP over the Democratic Party at a rate of 68 percent to 22 percent, according to Pew's survey. Whites in the South and working-class white men (those without a college degree) both favor the Republican Party by 21 percentage points.

Whites, however, make up a declining share of the electorate. Eighty-five percent of voters in the 1988 presidential election were white, according to the Roper Center for Public Opinion Research. In 2012 that figure stood at 72 percent.

Meanwhile, the proportion of African-American voters increased from 10 percent in 1988 to 13 percent in 2012. The Hispanic share of

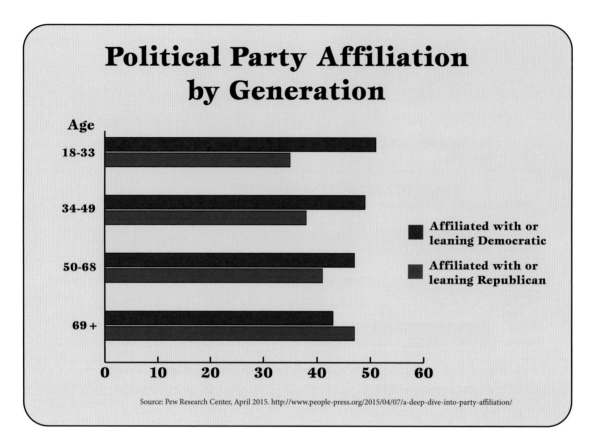

Political Party Affiliation by Generation

Age

18-33

34-49

50-68

69 +

Affiliated with or leaning Democratic

Affiliated with or leaning Republican

0   10   20   30   40   50   60

Source: Pew Research Center, April 2015. http://www.people-press.org/2015/04/07/a-deep-dive-into-party-affiliation/

the electorate jumped from 3 percent to 10 percent. Both of these groups overwhelmingly align with the Democratic Party—blacks by a 69-point margin, and Hispanics by a 30-point margin, according to the Pew Research Center. Latinos are of special concern for the GOP, as they already constitute the largest minority group in the United States and their numbers are increasing fast.

But the Republican Party also faces significant deficits in party identification among other major demographic groups. These include Asian Americans; women, particularly those who aren't married; people with no religious affiliation; and younger voters.

Many Republican leaders acknowledge that their party must broaden its appeal with these key constituencies to compete in presidential elections. But there's little consensus on what's necessary to achieve that. Some simply advocate a change in tone, believing the GOP's rhetoric has been unduly harsh and condescending. "If we continue to come across as people who are shrill, and who don't like people who disagree with us," notes former Republican National Committee chairman Haley Barbour, "we're going to be a very small party." Others, however, think the GOP must abandon some of its most conservative positions so that, as the political commentator David Frum writes, Republican candidates aren't "forced to contort themselves and embrace messages that must-win constituencies [find] deeply obnoxious." The adoption of more moderate positions, though, would risk alienating conservative base voters.

ISSUES: WHAT REPUBLICANS TODAY BELIEVE

No summary of what Republicans believe can be completely satisfactory. Large groups—and millions of Americans are Republicans—invariably accommodate a range of beliefs. Nevertheless, rank-and-file members of the Republican Party are generally distinguishable from their Democratic counterparts in the way they view government. Republicans today tend to have less faith in the federal government's ability to solve problems, and they typically advocate for smaller government.

Those general conclusions are supported by a vast amount of polling, including the Pew Research Center's Values Study. As part of that project, Pew has been collecting data about Americans' political values—including attitudes toward government, the economy, race, immigrants, the social safety net and the poor, and the environment—since 1987.

In 2012 Pew's American Values Survey found that 77 percent of Republicans believed programs run by the government are usually inefficient and wasteful. An identical percentage said the federal government controls too much of people's daily lives. By contrast, only 41 percent of Democrats judged government-run programs to be typically inefficient and wasteful, and 47 percent considered government control of citizens' daily lives excessive.

In 1988 the American Values Survey found that 68 percent of Republicans considered it the government's responsibility to take care of citizens unable to take care of themselves. By 2012 that figure had dropped to 40 percent, with only 36 percent saying the government should guarantee everyone enough to eat and a place to sleep. More than 9 in 10 Republicans (91 percent) said poor people had become too dependent on government assistance. Meanwhile, about three-quarters of Democrats said government is responsible for taking care of those who can't take care of themselves, and that it should ensure everyone enough food and a place to sleep; 57 percent said the poor had become too dependent on government aid programs.

Where business is concerned, most Republicans don't like government regulation. At the same time, many don't hold large corporations in high esteem either. In 2012 more than three-quarters (76 percent) of Republicans said that government regulation usually does more harm than good—the highest figure recorded on that particular question in the history of the American Values Survey. Fewer than half (47 percent) said a free market economy requires regulation by the government to best serve the public interest. Yet a solid majority of Republicans believed that too much power is concentrated in the hands of a few large companies (62 percent).

The GOP has long been an antitax party. In an April 2014 Gallup Organization poll, 57 percent of Republicans said the federal income tax they paid was too high, and 38 percent said that it was about right. That was practically a mirror image of what Democrats thought (too high: 37 percent; about right: 55 percent). Only small percentages from either party considered their own taxes too low (1 percent for Republicans, 5 percent for Democrats). But Democrats show much more willingness to have taxes raised on the wealthy and on corporations. In a 2014 Pew survey, 75 percent of Democrats but only 29 percent of Republicans said they'd favor such tax hikes to pay for antipoverty programs—confirmation, many in the GOP would argue, of Democrats' penchant for "redistributing wealth," a common criticism leveled by conservatives. About 6 in 10 Republicans in the 2014 Pew survey advocated lowering taxes on the rich and on corporations. This, they believed, would fuel economic growth—and ultimately help the poor.

When compared with Democrats, Republicans are less likely to consider environmental protection a major priority, especially if

Democratic vs. Republican Views on Current Issues

What is more important—to protect the right of Americans to own guns, OR to control gun ownership?

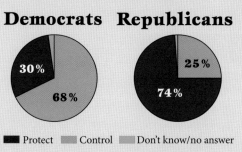

Democrats   Republicans

30% 68%   25% 74%

■ Protect   ■ Control   ■ Don't know/no answer

Should immigrants living in the U.S. illegally not be eligible for citizenship, OR be eligible for citizenship if they meet certain requirements?

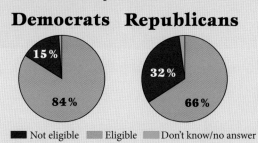

Democrats   Republicans

15% 84%   32% 66%

■ Not eligible   ■ Eligible   ■ Don't know/no answer

Do you think the federal government should ensure that all Americans have health care coverage, OR is that not the responsibility of the government?

Democrats   Republicans

28% 69%   18% 80%

■ Not responsibility   ■ Should ensure
■ Don't know/no answer

Overall, do you approve OR disapprove of the government's collection of telephone and internet data as part of anti-terrorism efforts?

Democrats   Republicans

49% 47%   58% 39%

■ Disapprove   ■ Approve   ■ Don't know/no answer

Do you think abortion should be illlegal OR legal in all or most cases?

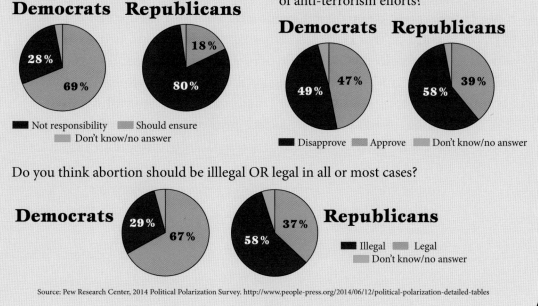

Democrats

29% 67%

58% 37%

Republicans

■ Illegal   ■ Legal
■ Don't know/no answer

Source: Pew Research Center, 2014 Political Polarization Survey. http://www.people-press.org/2014/06/12/political-polarization-detailed-tables

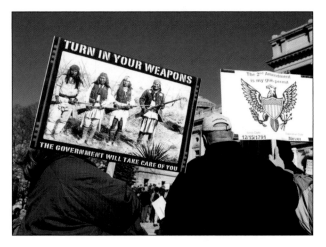

Most Republicans oppose stricter laws on firearm ownership in the United States.

economic costs are factored in. According to a Pew Research Center poll conducted January–March 2014, about 6 in 10 (59 percent) of Republicans believed stricter environmental laws weren't worth the economic harm they would presumably bring, including lost jobs. Seven in 10 Democrats, by contrast, said stricter environmental laws would be worth the cost. In another Pew survey, administered in January 2015, just 15 percent of Republicans said dealing with climate change should be a top priority for Congress and the president. A majority of Democrats (54 percent) said that it should.

On a range of social issues, GOP supporters remain decidedly more conservative than their Democratic counterparts. In 2015, for example: a Gallup poll found just 27 percent of Republicans in favor of stricter gun laws (Democrats in favor: 77 percent); in another Gallup poll, 76 percent of Republicans said the death penalty is morally acceptable (Democrats: 43 percent); and a Pew survey found 34 percent of Republicans in favor of legal recognition for same-sex marriage (Democrats: 65 percent).

Chapter 2

The GOP in the Reagan Era

In the modern history of the Republican Party, one figure towers above the rest: Ronald Wilson Reagan. A former movie actor and two-term governor of California, Reagan became the 40th president of the United States in 1981. As even his critics acknowledge, he fundamentally altered the political landscape of the United States. "I think Ronald Reagan changed the trajectory of America," Barack Obama, then a Democratic candidate for president, observed in 2008. Reagan brought conservative ideas to the forefront, and his vision of limited government ultimately displaced the big-government liberalism that had dominated national politics since the New Deal in the 1930s.

Today, nearly three decades after Reagan left office, his legacy remains powerful. Political debates over the proper scope of the government are still largely conducted on terms he set. Democrats have struggled to counter his message that the federal government is bloated, incompetent, and overbearing and should be shrunk.

For today's GOP, Ronald Reagan is like the North Star—always pointing to the right course, both for the party and for the country as a whole. Republican leaders invoke his name constantly. Often they claim he'd approve of a specific policy, which is presumed to settle the question of whether that policy is appropriate. Often they blame setbacks, for their party or for the country, on a failure to follow the course Reagan charted. They routinely depict that course as one of unswerving conservatism. But the 40th president's actual record is considerably more nuanced.

ENTER, "THE GREAT COMMUNICATOR"

Ronald Reagan had sought the Republican Party's nomination for president in 1968 and again in 1976. But he fell short both times. In 1980, however, he easily secured the nomination.

These weren't the best of times for the United States. The economy was in recession for much of 1980. As would be expected in an economic downturn, unemployment was high. But so was inflation, which added to Americans' economic insecurity. Overseas, Iranian militants had overrun the U.S. Embassy in Tehran and were holding 52 Americans hostage. A mission to free the hostages had failed, with eight American servicemen losing their lives in the process. Iran's leaders seemed to delight in humiliating the United States.

The Democratic president, Jimmy Carter, had acknowledged that the country was in the midst of a "crisis of confidence." But he appeared incapable of convincing Americans that the future would be better. Reagan, on the other hand, offered an optimistic vision. And he did so in a way that connected with ordinary Americans. It wasn't for nothing that he was hailed as the "Great Communicator." President Carter and the Democrats, Reagan declared in accepting the GOP's presidential nomination,

> say that the United States has had its day in the sun; that our nation has passed its zenith. They expect you to tell your children that the American people no longer have the will to cope with their problems; that the future will be one of sacrifice and few opportunities.
>   My fellow citizens, I utterly reject that view.

Reagan promised to reinvigorate the economy. He pledged to restore American military power, which he said was "at its lowest ebb in a generation." American voters responded to Reagan's confident and conservative message. In November 1980, he defeated Carter by a popular-vote margin of 51 percent to 41 percent.

ECONOMIC MATTERS

In his inaugural address on January 20, 1981, President Reagan blamed "unnecessary and excessive growth of government" for the nation's current difficulties. "In this present crisis," he declared, "government is not the solution to our problem; government is the problem." He pledged to curb the federal government's size and influence.

That goal featured prominently in the economic blueprint the White House submitted to Congress in February. Titled *America's New Beginning: A Program for Economic Recovery*, it called for reductions in federal spending and an easing of government regulations affecting business. The centerpiece, though, was an across-the-board tax cut of 30 percent (10 percent per year for three years) for all individual taxpayers. Changes to the tax code would also result in lower taxes for corporations.

Under a theory known as supply-side economics, the administration argued that the tax cuts wouldn't create big budget deficits for the federal government. Rather, administration officials said, the cuts would pay for themselves. The assumption was that reducing tax rates—particularly on high earners—would create an incentive for people to work more and invest more, unleashing a wave of new economic activity. More economic activity, in turn, would lead to more tax receipts for the government and greater prosperity for all of society.

Many Democrats were skeptical. They thought "Reaganomics," as the president's economic policies were dubbed, would overwhelmingly benefit those at the top of the income scale, with only meager gains going to the middle class and the poor.

President Reagan's extraordinary ability to connect with the American people earned him the nickname "the Great Communicator."

Democrats derisively referred to the president's supply-side approach as "trickle-down economics." They also objected to Reagan's proposed spending cuts, which targeted social programs—especially in light of the fact that the president was simultaneously pushing for huge increases in military spending.

While the 1980 elections had given the GOP control of the U.S. Senate, Democrats held the majority in the House of Representatives. The future of the Reagan administration's economic agenda seemed uncertain.

On March 30, 1981, President Reagan was shot and seriously wounded in an assassination attempt. His grace during that extremity—"I hope you're a Republican," he reportedly quipped as a surgeon was preparing to operate on him—and his gritty recovery from his wounds generated enormous goodwill.

By summer, polls showed that two-thirds of Americans approved of the president's economic plan. With broad bipartisan support, Congress passed the Economic Recovery Tax Act (ERTA), which provided for tax cuts that were only slightly lower than the White House economic blueprint had proposed. President Reagan signed ERTA into law on August 13, 1981.

The economy, however, was slipping back into recession. The downturn would last until November 1982, with the unemployment rate eventually climbing to 10.8 percent—3 points higher than the peak during the 1980 recession under the Carter administration.

At the same time, the Reagan administration faced another worrisome situation: the federal budget deficit was exploding. In order to address the shortfall, fiscally conservative Republicans in Congress urged the president to cancel some of the planned tax cuts in his 1983 national budget proposal.

Eventually, the president relented. He lobbied Congress to pass the Tax Equity and Fiscal Responsibility Act (TEFRA), which would effectively repeal about one-third of the scheduled tax cuts under ERTA. Critics, including Republicans, blasted the bill as the largest tax increase in history. Most Republicans in the House of Representatives voted against the final bill, but it passed with Democratic support. GOP defections in the Senate weren't as significant, but nine Democrats crossed the aisle to provide a slim margin for passage. President Reagan signed TEFRA into law on September 3, 1982.

Over the course of his presidency, Reagan would sign off on numerous other tax increases. In November 1982, for example, he agreed to a hike in the gasoline tax, to fund transportation projects. In April 1983, as part of a compromise worked out with Tip O'Neill, the Democratic Speaker of the House, he approved of payroll-tax increases to shore up the finances of Social Security (the government program providing income for retirees and the disabled). The Tax Reform Act of 1986, commonly thought of as Reagan's second tax cut, was actually a mix of tax reductions and tax increases.

In short, while Reagan was by nature an antitax conservative, he was also a pragmatist. "Ronald Reagan was never afraid to raise taxes," notes historian Douglas Brinkley, who edited the 40th president's diaries. "He knew that it was necessary at times."

That, however, wasn't the lesson many conservative Republicans would draw from the Reagan presidency. In part, that's because Reagan's rhetoric around taxes (and the excesses of the federal government generally) remained more unyielding than his actual approach. In 1985 Republican activist Grover Norquist founded an organization called Americans for Tax Reform. At the request of President Reagan, Norquist in 1986 drew up the "Taxpayer Protection Pledge," which Republican officeholders and candidates were pressured to sign. It bound them to "oppose and vote against any and all efforts to increase taxes."

IMBALANCED BUDGETS

If "the Pledge" was initially conceived as a way to constrain taxation, many conservative activists came to believe (incorrectly, as events demonstrated) that it would serve a broader purpose: shrinking the federal government by starving Washington of funds. "I don't want to abolish government," Norquist famously said. "I simply want to reduce it to the size where I can drag it into the bathroom and drown it in the bathtub."

That was something Ronald Reagan never managed to do, in spite of all his limited-government rhetoric. By virtually any measure, the federal government expanded during his presidency. The federal workforce grew by about 300,000. Spending increased steadily. Budget deficits soared and the national debt nearly tripled.

Supporters argue that with Democrats in control of the House of Representatives (and, after 1986, the Senate), President Reagan couldn't possibly obtain the spending cuts he wanted. And that's certainly true. But it's only part of the story.

The first budget proposal Reagan submitted to Congress, for fiscal year 1982, did contain substantial spending cuts. It was, in fact, nearly 6 percent smaller than the proposed budget of President Carter. Reagan had long argued that government social-welfare programs sap personal initiative and foster dependency. His budget called for, and Congress accepted, cuts to various programs—from food stamps and school lunches to public housing and Medicaid (government-funded health care for the poor). Such programs didn't have politically powerful constituencies, and the cuts provoked relatively little controversy.

The situation was different when the administration called for major cuts to early retirement benefits under Social Security. A massive hue and cry resulted—Social Security being a broadly popular entitlement—and Reagan's favorability plummeted. After that experience, biographer Lou Cannon notes, Reagan "would never again mount a major assault against the basic premises of the federal budget." Instead he "was reduced to tinkering at the margins of entitlements," tacitly accepting that federal spending would grow—and the budget would not be balanced during his presidency.

ELECTIONS

Democrats made political hay of the administration's proposal to slash Social Security benefits. In the 1982 congressional midterms, the GOP lost 26 seats in the House of Representatives.

By January 1983, Gallup polling showed President Reagan's job approval at just 35 percent. Many political observers believed the president's reelection prospects were dim. But in 1983 the U.S. economy

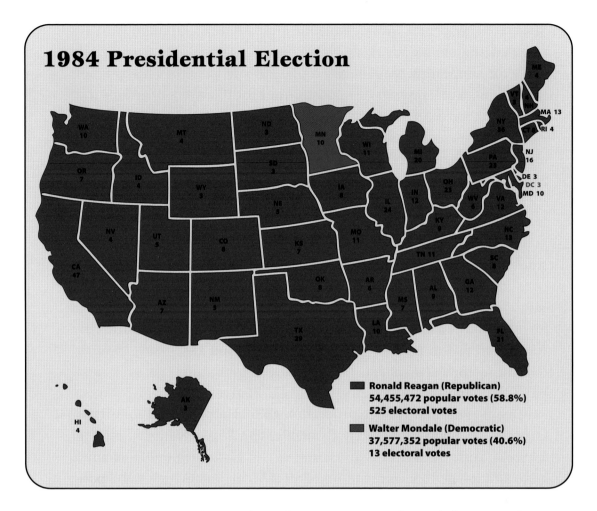

1984 Presidential Election

Ronald Reagan (Republican)
54,455,472 popular votes (58.8%)
525 electoral votes

Walter Mondale (Democratic)
37,577,352 popular votes (40.6%)
13 electoral votes

rebounded strongly, and with it Reagan's favorability numbers. Robust economic growth continued in 1984.

The Democratic Party's 1984 presidential nominee, Walter Mondale, argued that Reagan's policies had helped the rich but left working people behind. And Mondale, who'd served as vice president under Jimmy Carter, said taxes would have to be raised to deal with the burgeoning national debt.

Voters rejected that message. In the 1984 presidential election Reagan trounced Mondale, carrying 49 states and winning the popular vote by 18 percent.

The magnitude of Reagan's victory was made possible by his ability to attract groups that had typically voted Democratic. Among these

"Reagan Democrats" were working-class whites. Opinion surveys revealed that many working-class whites resented the Democratic Party for supporting racially based policies such as affirmative action (actively seeking to promote opportunities for members of groups that have historically suffered discrimination, such as African Americans). Such policies, many working-class whites believed, unfairly disadvantaged them, and Reagan's stated opposition to all forms of "reverse discrimination" resonated deeply.

In what they call a "momentous achievement," political scientists Earl Black and Merle Black also credit Reagan with completing the political realignment of the South. In a trend that had been under way since the 1960s, white southerners—previously a solid Democratic constituency—increasingly gravitated toward Republican presidential candidates. Reagan's overwhelming popularity helped accelerate a broader shift in partisan loyalties among whites in the South. "By transforming the region's electorate," Black and Black say, "Ronald Reagan's presidency made possible the Republicans' congressional breakthrough in the 1990s."

During Reagan's time in office, though, his popularity didn't translate into a big boost for the GOP overall. The Republicans did pick up 16 seats in the House of Representatives in 1984, but the Democrats were still left with a commanding 253–182 majority. Meanwhile, the GOP lost two seats in the Senate but still retained a majority. In the 1986 midterm elections, the Democrats gained eight Senate seats to win control of both chambers of Congress.

ENDING THE COLD WAR

Since the late 1940s the United States and the Soviet Union, a Communist superpower, had been locked in a struggle for global influence known as the Cold War. President Reagan organized his foreign policy around one principal goal: rolling back the reach of Soviet communism.

To achieve that goal, Reagan believed it necessary to exert military pressure on the Soviet Union, which he characterized as an "evil empire." He oversaw the largest peacetime military buildup in U.S.

history, with annual defense expenditures more than doubling between 1980 and 1985. Tens of billions of dollars were invested in new high-tech weapons systems. "It was a matter of demonstrating to [the Soviets]," noted Secretary of Defense Caspar Weinberger, "that they couldn't win a war" with the United States. Meanwhile, under what came to be called the Reagan Doctrine, the United States funneled aid to anticommunist rebels around the world.

In November 1983 the North Atlantic Treaty Organization—a military alliance consisting of the United States, Canada, and various Western European nations—conducted a sprawling nuclear-weapons command exercise. Some Soviet leaders worried that the United States intended to use the NATO maneuvers to launch an actual nuclear attack on the Soviet Union. Certain Soviet units were evidently preparing a preemptive nuclear strike. The incident left President Reagan deeply shaken. "I began to realize," he later admitted, "that many Soviet officials feared us not only as adversaries but as potential aggressors who might hurl nuclear weapons at them in a first strike." That situation raised the risk of a catastrophic miscalculation on the part of the Soviets.

Reagan sought to reassure Soviet leaders. He urgently called for the resumption of negotiations to reduce stockpiles of nuclear warheads and missiles.

The president would find a willing negotiating partner after Mikhail Gorbachev ascended to the Soviet Union's top leadership post in March 1985. The new Soviet premier was eager to reform his country politically and economically, and he considered better relations with the United States vital to that effort.

In October 1986, Gorbachev and Reagan discussed ideas for dramatically reducing the U.S. and Soviet nuclear arsenals at a hastily arranged summit in Reykjavik, Iceland. No formal agreement emerged, but the Reykjavik meeting marked a turning point. Reagan and Gorbachev realized that they shared the goal of nuclear disarmament. And when he returned home, Gorbachev reported to the rest of the Soviet leadership that the United States really didn't harbor any intentions of launching a nuclear first strike against the Soviet Union.

President Reagan shakes hands with Mikhail Gorbachev, general secretary of the Soviet Union's Communist Party, after the signing of a nuclear-missile treaty in 1988. Reagan administration policies are widely credited with hastening the collapse of communism in the Soviet Union and Eastern Europe, thus ending the Cold War.

A thaw in U.S.-Soviet relations ensued. This strengthened Gorbachev's hand at home, enabling the Soviet leader to proceed with his reform agenda.

Gorbachev's reforms, in turn, produced a chain of events that in 1989 led the Soviet Union to relinquish control of the Eastern European countries it had dominated since the early years of the Cold War. In 1991 the Soviet Union itself collapsed. Reagan had left office by the time this occurred, but there is little doubt his policies played a role in bringing the Cold War to a conclusion and, in the process, rolling back global communism.

That achievement helped solidify the Republican Party's reputation for tough, effective foreign policy. For the next 15 years, Americans would consistently regard the GOP as stronger on national defense and foreign policy than the Democratic Party.

Chapter 3

Shifting Political Fortunes

I n campaigning for the presidency in 1988, Vice President George H. W. Bush pledged to build on the successes of Ronald Reagan. Bush credited Republican policies for the healthy economy, which had been expanding for more than five years. He suggested that his Democratic opponent, Governor Michael Dukakis of Massachusetts, would raise taxes. That was something Bush categorically promised not to do. "Read my lips: no new taxes," he memorably said.

Bush also drew on themes that had proved effective for Reagan. His opponent, he claimed, believed that the country was on a long and inevitable path toward decline, whereas Bush knew that "America is a rising nation." Republicans seek to empower the individual, Bush said, but Democrats simply "want power in the hands of the federal government."

Social issues—in particular, crime—would play a major role in the campaign. Crime rates in the United States had risen dramatically since the 1960s, and many Americans favored a get-tough approach to criminals. Bush hammered Dukakis for opposing the death penalty, which he said was evidence the Massachusetts governor was "soft on crime." The Bush campaign found a potent symbol to drive home that

President George Bush is greeted by U.S. troops stationed in Saudi Arabia, 1990. Early the following year, these troops would be part of the U.S.-led coalition that defeated Iraq in the Gulf War. Polls taken in February 1991, as the war was ending, showed 89 percent of Americans approved of the job Bush was doing as president. However, by June 1992, amid a struggling American economy, the president's approval rating had fallen to 29 percent.

point on a visceral level. In 1986, while Dukakis was governor, a convicted murderer named Willie Horton had escaped from a weekend furlough program in Massachusetts and fled to Maryland, where he brutally assaulted a woman and her fiancé.

GEORGE H. W. BUSH: RISE AND FALL

During the summer of 1988, polls showed Bush trailing Dukakis by more than 15 points. But by November the tide had turned. With a particularly strong showing among white working-class voters, who made up more than half of the entire electorate, Bush breezed to victory. He won about 53 percent of the popular vote and swept the southern states on the way to amassing 426 votes in the Electoral College (270 are needed to claim the presidency).

The GOP didn't fare as well in the 1988 congressional elections, which saw Democrats make small gains in the Senate and House of Representatives and retain solid control of both chambers. Democrats would add to their congressional majorities in the 1990 midterms as well.

Foreign affairs occupied much of the Bush presidency. Arms control treaties were signed with the Soviet Union and, later, with Russia and several of the other independent countries that arose in the aftermath of the Soviet Union's breakup. In December 1989 President Bush ordered an invasion of Panama to apprehend dictator Manuel Noriega, who'd been indicted in the United States for drug trafficking.

A far larger military operation took place in the Middle East, after Iraq invaded and annexed neighboring Kuwait in August 1990. President Bush vowed that the aggression wouldn't be allowed to stand. And in the succeeding months, under authorization from the United Nations, his administration assembled an international coalition dedicated to expelling Iraqi forces from Kuwait. Some three dozen countries agreed to participate. It was an extraordinary diplomatic achievement, and it would be matched by success on the battlefield. On February 24, 1991, following a six-week air campaign, coalition ground forces—led by American units—attacked. Iraq's army was routed and Kuwait liberated in less than five days.

In the wake of the Gulf War, Bush's popularity soared. His approval rating, according to Gallup, reached an astronomical 89 percent—higher than any previous president had ever attained in the Gallup survey. Some political pundits suggested Bush was a shoo-in for reelection.

But the economy had slipped into a recession, and economic growth was sluggish even after the downturn ended. In addition, Bush had broken his pledge not to raise taxes. The 1991 budget he signed included about $140 billion in new taxes. The president said the revenue was needed to close the federal government's persistently large budget deficits, but the GOP's conservative wing was furious.

The Democratic Party's 1992 presidential nominee, Arkansas governor Bill Clinton, effectively capitalized on the weak state of the economy. He also deliberately positioned himself near the political center, even adopting rhetoric that wouldn't have

President Bush's plummeting popularity inspired Texas billionaire Ross Perot to mount an independent campaign for president in 1992.

1992 Presidential Election

George H.W. Bush (Republican)
39,104,550 popular votes (37.5%)
168 electoral votes

Bill Clinton (Democratic)
44,909,806 popular votes (43%)
370 electoral votes

Ross Perot (Patriot)
19,743,821 popular votes (18.9%)

sounded out of place coming from Ronald Reagan. "There is not a program in government for every problem," Clinton declared at the Democratic National Convention. In that same speech, he promised to "end welfare as we know it . . . because welfare should be a second chance, not a way of life."

On Election Day, many of the so-called Reagan Democrats returned to the Democratic Party. Clinton lost the white vote by just 2 percentage points. Meanwhile, he racked up huge majorities among African-American and Latino voters, providing him with a comfortable, 43 percent to 37 percent margin of victory over Bush in the popular vote. (Independent candidate H. Ross Perot, a billionaire businessman, garnered about 19 percent of the vote.) Clinton also broke the GOP's recent stranglehold on the South, winning Georgia, Louisiana, and Tennessee, in addition to his native Arkansas.

A RECESSION THAT DIDN'T MATERIALIZE

When Clinton took the oath of office in January 1993, the Democratic Party held commanding majorities in both the Senate and House of Representatives. Nevertheless, the president soon ran into trouble getting a budget through Congress, because it included tax increases on upper-income individuals and on corporations. Clinton insisted that the tax hikes were needed to shrink the still-gaping budget shortfall. Ultimately the Omnibus Budget Reconciliation Act of 1993 passed by a single vote in each chamber of Congress. Not one Republican voted in favor of the bill.

The consensus among GOP lawmakers was that the tax hikes would devastate the economy. "We are buying a one-way ticket to a recession," railed Senator Phil Gramm of Texas. His Republican colleague in the House, Georgia's Newt Gingrich, concurred. "The tax increase will kill jobs and lead to a recession," Gingrich predicted, "and the recession will force people off of work and onto unemployment and actually increase the deficit."

The Republicans' pessimism proved unfounded. The U.S. economy would continue expanding through the end of the decade, producing robust job growth. And the budget deficit decreased steadily, with the federal government running surpluses from 1998 to 2001.

None of that dampened Republicans' enthusiasm for supply-side economics. The GOP viewed reducing taxes as essential to driving economic growth, and over the years an overwhelming majority of Republicans in Congress would sign Grover Norquist's Taxpayer Protection Pledge.

THE REPUBLICAN REVOLUTION

By the late summer of 1994, with midterm elections looming, President Clinton's popularity was at an ebb. Americans had turned decisively against an initiative Clinton had intended to be the centerpiece of his administration: a plan to overhaul the nation's health care system and guarantee health insurance to all citizens. Many people thought the plan would lead to a big expansion of the federal bureaucracy while adversely affecting the quality of the health care they received. A Gallup survey conducted during the first week of September 1994 showed just 39 percent of Americans approved of the way Clinton was handling his job, while 54 percent disapproved.

Congress was viewed even less favorably: just 21 percent of Americans approved of the way it was doing its job, and 73 percent disapproved, according to a Gallup poll from the first week of October. A pair of ethics scandals had sullied the House of Representatives.

Americans were angry and frustrated with Washington, and Democrats got the lion's share of the blame. They were, after all, in control of Congress and the White House.

Newt Gingrich, the number-two GOP leader in the House, believed that Republicans could best capitalize on the anti-Washington sentiment by running on a unified platform. To that end, Gingrich unveiled the Contract with America. It outlined 10 bills the Republicans promised to introduce in the first 100 days of the new Congress if they won a majority. One of those bills would help "restore fiscal responsibility to an out-of-control Congress" by means of a constitutional amendment requiring a balanced budget and "tax limitation." Another would cut spending on welfare programs and prohibit single mothers under the age of 18 from receiving any benefits. Still another would mandate term limits, "to replace career politicians with citizen legislators."

The results on Election Day were astonishing: not a single incumbent Republican senator or representative was defeated. The GOP picked up eight seats in the Senate and 54 seats in the House, gaining control of both chambers of Congress for the first time in four decades. The press christened the GOP landslide "the Republican Revolution."

True to their word, Republicans brought the 10 bills in the Contract with America to the floor of the House in the first hundred days of the 104th Congress. Nine passed (the exception being the term-limits bill), but most of the legislation languished in the Senate.

OVERREACH

In the wake of the Republican Revolution, President Clinton promised to "do my dead level best" to work with the new GOP-controlled Congress. But the White House and Republican legislators—led by Speaker of the House Newt Gingrich—would engage in a series of rancorous fights.

Objecting to Republican-backed cuts in Medicaid and Medicare (the government health care program for the elderly), Clinton vetoed a short-term spending measure sent to him by Congress in November 1995. GOP legislators held firm, however, forcing a partial shutdown of the federal government that began November 14. Some 800,000 government employees were furloughed.

Gingrich publicly boasted that he'd provoked the shutdown in part as payback for a perceived slight by President Clinton. During a recent trip to Israel for the funeral of Prime Minister Yitzhak Rabin, Clinton hadn't talked to Gingrich on the return flight, and the Speaker had been asked to exit Air Force One from the rear ramp. "You just wonder," Gingrich complained, "where is their sense of manners?"

House Speaker Newt Gingrich (right) and Vice President Al Gore look on as President Clinton delivers the 1995 State of the Union Address. Gingrich, the leader of the 1994 Republican Revolution, engaged Clinton in a series of bitter political battles during the 1990s.

Bob Dole, the 1996 Republican nominee for president, delivers a campaign speech. Dole boasted an impressive record—he'd been a World War II hero, a five-term U.S. senator representing Kansas, and Senate majority leader. But with the U.S. economy booming, President Clinton easily won reelection, carrying 31 states plus the District of Columbia for an Electoral College margin of 379 to 159.

To many people, Gingrich came across as petty. Not surprisingly, opinion polls showed that significantly more Americans blamed Congress than the president for the government shutdown.

On November 19, the White House and congressional Republicans reached an agreement to end the shutdown. The government was to be funded through December 15. In addition, the president and Congress committed to enacting legislation that would balance the federal budget by 2002. But when the two parties failed to agree on the details of a seven-year balanced-budget plan, another shutdown ensued. This one began on December 16 and lasted six days into the new year.

In his 1996 State of the Union Address, Clinton appeared to concede much of the basic argument the GOP had been pressing since Ronald Reagan's presidency. "The era of big Government," he declared, "is over." But if he acknowledged that the federal government had to live within its means, Clinton also insisted that "we cannot go back to the time when our citizens were left to fend for themselves."

By summer, congressional Republicans and the White House had found common ground in the Personal Responsibility and Work Opportunity Act. The bill, which Clinton signed into law in August, set a lifetime limit of five years for welfare benefits and required able-bodied recipients to find employment.

In the November elections, the GOP kept control of Congress, but Clinton easily won another term. He beat Bob Dole of Kansas, the former Senate majority leader, by about 8 percent in the popular vote.

Republican lawmakers reached several significant compromises with the president during Clinton's second term. For example, the Balanced Budget Act of 1997 included reductions in spending on Medicare and Medicaid, which the GOP favored. But the act also established a new federal program that Clinton advocated—health insurance for children whose families earned too much to qualify for Medicaid but too little to afford private insurance.

One issue on which congressional Republicans and the president couldn't agree was what to do with budget surpluses, which were projected to continue through 2010. Republicans proposed large tax cuts, which Clinton rejected. He said most of the surpluses should be used to pay off the national debt.

Scandal was in the headlines throughout much of Clinton's second term as president. Kenneth Starr—an independent counsel originally charged with investigating an Arkansas real estate deal in which Bill Clinton and his wife, Hillary, had invested—began probing allegations that President Clinton hadn't been truthful in a deposition (a sworn statement) he gave for a sexual-harassment lawsuit. The allegations centered on Clinton's relationship with a White House intern named Monica Lewinsky. In August 1998, the president testified before a grand jury convened by the independent counsel. In a report issued the following month, Starr outlined 11 possible grounds on which Clinton could be impeached, including obstruction of justice and perjury (lying under oath).

Opinion surveys showed that, by an overwhelming margin, Americans didn't think the president should be impeached. For example, a CNN poll conducted in early October found 62 percent against impeachment, and just 34 percent in favor. Nevertheless, just weeks before midterm elections, the House Judiciary Committee voted to proceed with an impeachment investigation. Polling had indicated that the Republican Party was poised to make significant gains in Congress, but the GOP edge quickly dissipated.

One week before the elections, the Republicans unveiled an ad campaign that focused on the Clinton sex scandal and that was devised by Newt Gingrich. The gambit didn't work. On Election Day, there was no net change in the Senate; in the House the GOP lost five seats. Two days later, Gingrich announced his resignation as Speaker of the House.

On December 19, 1998, the House—on a mostly party-line vote—approved two articles of impeachment against President Clinton. One count involved obstruction of justice, and the other perjury.

On January 7, fulfilling its constitutional responsibility, the Senate opened the impeachment trial of President Clinton. If two-thirds of the senators voted to convict the president on either article of impeachment, he would be removed from office.

The nation's second-ever presidential impeachment came to an end on February 12, 1999. That day, the Senate acquitted Clinton. The vote on the perjury charge was 45 in favor of conviction and 55 in favor of acquittal; the vote on the obstruction of justice count was split 50–50.

"The GOP is standing in quicksand," Senator Ben Nighthorse Campbell, a Republican from Colorado, remarked in the aftermath of the impeachment trial. Campbell, like many political observers, believed American voters would punish the Republican Party for trying to hound Clinton from office over a sex scandal. But the next national elections were more than 20 months away—an eternity in politics.

Chapter 4

Troubled Times

I n 2000 George W. Bush won the Republican presidential primary race easily. Bush, the son of former president George H. W. Bush, was a popular two-term governor of Texas. He recognized that the GOP had in recent years gained a reputation for being harsh and uncaring, particularly toward the needy. "People think oftentimes that Republicans are mean-spirited folks," Bush told an interviewer.

He promised a different approach: "compassionate conservatism." Like garden-variety conservatism, this idea assumed that the federal bureaucracy was ill equipped to deal with social problems such as poverty. However, that didn't absolve the government of the obligation to help the disadvantaged. It simply meant that, rather than providing social services directly, the government should (where possible) fund the initiatives of private charities, faith-based organizations, and community groups—and to insist on "accountability and results."

Bush's vision for compassionate conservatism would never be realized in any comprehensive way. Yet in the view of some political observers—such as conservative writer Reihan Salam and Bush adviser David Gerson—it helped him win the presidency in 2000.

The 2000 presidential election was one of the closest—and most contentious—in U.S. history. Vice President Al Gore, the Democratic

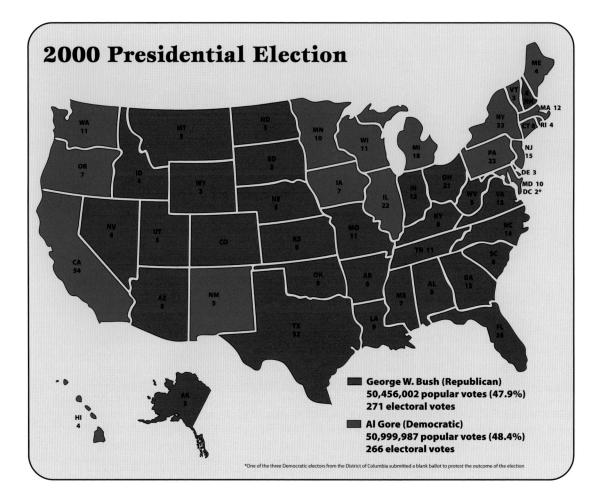

2000 Presidential Election

WA 11
MT 3
ND 3
MN 10
WI 11
MI 18
ME 4
VT 3
NH
MA 12
NY 33
CT 8 RI 4
OR 7
ID 4
WY 3
SD 3
IA 7
IL 22
IN 12
OH 21
PA 23
NJ 15
DE 3
MD 10
DC 2*
NV 4
UT 5
CO
NE 5
MO 11
KY 8
WV 5
VA 13
NC 14
CA 54
AZ 8
NM 5
KS 6
OK 8
AR 6
TN 11
MS 7
AL 9
GA 13
SC 8
TX 32
LA 9
FL 25
AK 3
HI 4

George W. Bush (Republican)
50,456,002 popular votes (47.9%)
271 electoral votes

Al Gore (Democratic)
50,999,987 popular votes (48.4%)
266 electoral votes

*One of the three Democratic electors from the District of Columbia submitted a blank ballot to protest the outcome of the election

Party candidate, topped Bush in the nationwide popular vote by about five-tenths of 1 percent. However, the outcome in Florida—where the popular-vote margin came down to a few thousandths of 1 percent—was disputed. And without winning the Sunshine State, neither candidate could reach the threshold of 270 electoral votes necessary to claim the presidency. On December 12, with Bush holding a razor-thin lead in the official popular-vote tally, the U.S. Supreme Court overturned a decision by the Florida State Supreme Court ordering a vote recount. This ensured that Bush would become the 43rd president of the United States.

When President Bush first took office in January 2001, his party had control in both chambers of Congress. The 2000 elections had left the GOP clinging to a narrow 221–212 majority in the House. The Senate was split 50–50—Republicans having lost four seats—but the GOP would enjoy effective control because the Constitution empowers the vice president to cast the deciding vote in the event a Senate vote is tied. In June, however, Senator Jim Jeffords of Vermont left the GOP, giving the Democratic Party the slimmest of majorities.

CUTTING TAXES, EXPANDING ENTITLEMENTS

President Bush succeeded in getting several major domestic initiatives enacted during his first years in office. In June 2001, he signed into law the Economic Growth and Tax Relief Reconciliation Act (EGTRRA), which lowered the income-tax rates most Americans paid. EGTRRA also reduced the estate tax (which benefited wealthier families) and increased the earned income tax credit (which benefited lower-income families). Further tax cuts were contained in the Jobs and Growth Tax Relief Reconciliation Act (JGTRRA), which Bush signed in May 2003. Among other provisions, JGTRRA reduced the tax rate on dividends (money paid regularly to shareholders in a company) and capital gains (profits from the sale of property or an investment).

EGTRRA and JGTRRA both passed Congress with near-unanimous GOP support and overwhelming Democratic opposition. Democrats complained that the tax cuts disproportionately benefited the wealthy and would lead to big budget deficits. According to Senator Joseph Liebermann of Connecticut, the president's policies had the effect of "giving the most to those who need it least [and] piling more debt on the backs of our children." Republicans countered that the tax cuts would stimulate enough eco-

Fiscal conservatives generally praised Bush's tax cuts, but his administration received criticism for increasing the size of the federal government.

nomic activity to ultimately pay for themselves. "By giving individuals more money to spend and also creating more jobs in the economy," noted Tennessee Republican Bill Frist, the Senate majority leader, "we will be able to grow that economy, which over time will make [the] deficit disappear."

If tax cutting is a pillar of the modern GOP's agenda, expanding entitlement programs is not. But in 2003 President Bush pushed for—and Congress passed—what the conservative historian and former Reagan aide Bruce Bartlett decried as "the largest expansion of the welfare state since the creation of Medicare in 1965." The Medicare Prescription Drug, Improvement, and Modernization Act subsidized the cost of prescription medications for recipients of Medicare. The idea itself had broad bipartisan support. But the bill prohibited the government from negotiating drug costs with pharmaceutical manufacturers, which caused most Democrats to vote against it. And some Republicans, especially in the House of Representatives, balked because the cost of the new prescription drug benefit wasn't offset by spending cuts. Nevertheless, the GOP leadership managed to push the bill through the House under controversial circumstances, and President Bush signed it into law on December 8, 2003.

Even before then, the federal government's budget surpluses had evaporated. One factor was a recession lasting from March to November 2001. Another was the tax cuts. Still another was the costs of war.

"WAR ON TERROR"

On September 11, 2001, terrorists belonging to a group called al-Qaeda hijacked four U.S. passenger airliners. Two of the planes were flown into the World Trade Center in New York City, and another was flown into the Pentagon, outside Washington, D.C. The fourth plane crashed in southwestern Pennsylvania following a struggle between passengers and the hijackers. In all, about 3,000 people lost their lives in the attacks.

With only one dissenting vote, Congress quickly passed a joint resolution authorizing the president "to use all necessary and appropriate force against those nations, organizations, or persons he determines planned, authorized, committed, or aided the terrorist attacks."

For his part, Bush promised that "our war on terror begins with Al Qaeda, but it does not end there. It will not end until every terrorist group of global reach has been found, stopped and defeated."

In October 2001, U.S. forces—joined by British troops—attacked

In the weeks after the September 11 attacks, most Americans supported President Bush's declaration of a "war on terror."

Afghanistan. That country's government, known as the Taliban, was harboring al-Qaeda leader Osama bin Laden and many of the terrorist group's fighters. Although the Taliban was quickly overthrown, bin Laden escaped into neighboring Pakistan.

By the late summer of 2002, the Bush administration was signaling that the "war on terror" might have to be expanded into another country. Iraq, the president said, "possesses and produces chemical and biological weapons. It is seeking nuclear weapons. It has given shelter and support to terrorism." If the Iraqi regime of Saddam Hussein did indeed have or was trying to obtain so-called weapons of mass destruction (WMD)—chemical, biological, or nuclear weapons—that would violate the cease-fire terms the United Nations had imposed on Iraq after the 1991 Gulf War.

In October 2002, Congress passed a joint resolution authorizing the use of military force against Iraq if Saddam's regime failed to comply with its disarmament obligations. Only one GOP senator and six Republicans in the House voted against the use-of-force resolution, but Democrats were deeply divided.

Secretary of Defense Donald Rumsfeld (left) meets with President George W. Bush and Vice President Dick Cheney to discuss the "war on terrorism." The Bush administration claimed that Iraq posed a potential danger to the United States that required the removal of Saddam Hussein from power.

Although exit polling in the 2002 midterm elections showed that few Americans considered Iraq a major issue, President Bush was immensely popular, and more than one-third of voters said they cast their votes to show support for him. Republicans padded their majority in the House by picking up eight seats. They also regained control of the Senate by netting two additional seats.

Throughout late 2002 and early 2003, the Bush administration pressed the case that Saddam Hussein's regime presented a growing threat to the United States and its allies, emphasizing in particular Iraq's supposed efforts to develop nuclear weapons. The president claimed not to have made a final decision on whether a war would be necessary to disarm Iraq. In the event it was, however, administration officials insisted that the conflict would be brief and inexpensive. That was premised on the assumption that ordinary Iraqis wouldn't regard American and allied troops as foreign occupiers but would instead be grateful for the overthrow of Saddam Hussein's brutal dictatorship. "I really do believe that we will be greeted as liberators," Vice President Dick Cheney declared, dismissing a journalist's question about what would happen if a U.S. invasion force encountered widespread popular resistance.

MIRAGE OF VICTORY

On March 19, 2003, as U.S. cruise missiles pounded the capital city of Baghdad, President Bush announced that war with Iraq had begun. Initially, the conflict appeared to unfold as the administration had predicted. By mid-April, American troops had secured Baghdad, and organized resistance from the Iraqi army had virtually ceased. "Major combat operations in Iraq have ended," Bush declared on May 1. "In the battle of Iraq, the United States and our allies have prevailed."

That declaration of victory turned out to be tragically premature. In the months and years that followed, Iraq descended into chaos—with former members of Saddam Hussein's disbanded army and dissolved ruling party mounting a violent insurgency, al-Qaeda taking root in Iraq, and a savage civil war erupting between Iraq's Sunni Muslim minority and its Shia Muslim majority.

U.S. Marines on patrol in Fallujah, Iraq, 2004. The initial invasion of Iraq was relatively smooth, with the government of Saddam Hussein falling in a matter of weeks. But the Bush administration seriously underestimated the difficulties of maintaining order in the aftermath. American troops would spend years battling an insurgency, struggling to suppress violence between Iraq's rival religious and ethnic factions, and fighting terrorists aligned with al-Qaeda.

Anti-war protesters march though Santa Barbara, California, in March 2007. By this time the continued involvement of the U.S. military in Iraq had grown highly unpopular with the American public. In March 2007 just 35 percent of Americans approved of the job Bush was doing as president. By the time of the presidential election the next year, that number had dropped even further, to 25 percent.

In spite of the deteriorating situation in Iraq—and the failure to find any WMD there—Republicans fared well in the 2004 elections. The GOP picked up three seats in the House and four in the Senate. By a popular-vote margin of just under 2.5 percent, President Bush won reelection over his Democratic challenger, Senator John Kerry of Massachusetts. Exit polls showed that more voters considered Bush a strong leader and believed he'd do a better job of prosecuting the "war on terror." The Iraq War was largely neutralized as an effective campaign issue for Kerry because he'd voted for the resolution authorizing military force.

But Iraq would bedevil Bush during his second term in office. Amid mounting American casualties and no clear way out of the morass, Bush's favorability steadily declined—and so did that of the GOP.

By the time the 2006 midterm elections arrived, opinion polls showed that a solid majority of Americans considered the Iraq War a mistake. And the Republican Party paid the price, losing 30 seats in the House of Representatives and six seats in the Senate. Democrats had gained control of both chambers of Congress.

Chapter 5

"Figuring Out What Comes Next"

The 2008 presidential campaign took place against a backdrop of national angst. In a NBC News/*Wall Street Journal* poll conducted on the eve of the election, 76 percent said the country was on the wrong track, while just 11 percent said it was on the right track.

Although a U.S. troop "surge" had succeeded in tamping down the violence in Iraq somewhat, the situation there remained unstable, and American soldiers continued to be killed. But opinion surveys showed that Iraq wasn't what worried the American public most. The economy was. The country was in the midst of a severe recession, with rising unemployment and a meltdown of the financial sector.

The presidential race pitted Republican John McCain, a four-term U.S. senator from Arizona, against Democrat Barack Obama, a freshman senator from Illinois. Polling indicated that McCain was hurt by the perception that he'd continue the policies of George W. Bush, whose favorability had cratered. Obama promised sweeping change— and not just in the policy realm. He pledged to change what he characterized as Washington's broken, overly partisan politics.

Obama defeated McCain handily, winning the popular vote by about 7 percentage points. Meanwhile, Democrats substantially increased their majorities in both the House and the Senate. For the

43

first time since 1994, the GOP wouldn't control either chamber of Congress or the White House.

THE WAY BACK

GOP leaders soon began planning a comeback. On January 20, 2009—the day of Obama's inauguration—a group of top Republicans held a strategy session. According to journalist Robert Draper, who chronicled the meeting in his book *Do Not Ask What Good We Do*, the Republican leaders decided that the key to regaining power would be to stifle the agenda of the new president and the Democratic Congress. And to do that they'd have to be united in opposition. "Everyone's got to stick together," observed Representative Paul Ryan of Wisconsin, a rising star in the GOP.

"If you act like you're the minority," added Representative Kevin McCarthy of California, "you're going to stay in the minority. We've gotta challenge them on every single bill and every single campaign."

Before long, evidence of the GOP's strategy of unified opposition to the president had emerged. With the economy in a virtual free fall—U.S. job losses in January 2009 were higher than in any single month since 1974—Obama proposed an economic-stimulus package that would increase federal spending and cut taxes. Previously, those had been widely accepted ways for the government to foster demand and boost employment to combat a recession. But Republicans complained that, at nearly $800 billion, the cost of the American Recovery and Reinvestment Act (ARRA) was too high. Not a single GOP House member voted for the bill. In the Senate, only three Republicans broke ranks with their party.

ARRA, which President Obama signed into law on February 17, was just one of several large federal programs designed to deal with the economic crisis. Others included a bailout of major financial institutions and a bailout of two floundering auto manufacturers, General Motors and Chrysler.

With the national debt already at $10 trillion, some Americans seethed at the new round of federal spending. Anger crystallized in the Tea Party movement, whose members demanded a return to budg-

Protesters attend a "Tea Party" rally in St. Louis a month before the 2010 midterm elections. The Tea Party is a conservative political movement whose members, polling shows, overwhelmingly identify with the GOP. A core belief of the Tea Party movement is that the federal government has grown too large and powerful.

etary discipline and the kind of limited government, including low taxes, they believed the Constitution requires. In opinion surveys, large majorities of Tea Party supporters identified themselves as conservatives, and large majorities said they were either Republican or leaned Republican. But many Tea Party members were disillusioned with the GOP establishment, which they thought had betrayed conservative principles.

Nonetheless, the Tea Party proved a potent ally in Republican efforts to thwart President Obama's agenda. During the summer of 2009, Tea Party groups around the country angrily protested Obama's major health care reform initiative, saying it was symptomatic of the out-of-control federal government and a threat to individual liberty.

However, despite unanimous Republican opposition in Congress, the Patient Protection and Affordable Care Act—popularly known as Obamacare—ultimately passed. The president signed it into law in March 2010. But the entire process had enraged and energized conservatives.

Three people who'd been at the GOP strategy session of January 20, 2009—Ryan, McCarthy, and Representative Eric Cantor of Virginia—spearheaded efforts to recruit Tea Party members to run for House seats in 2010. They pledged to immediately slash $100 billion in federal spending if the Republican Party gained the majority. They urged their recruits to run on the promise of repealing Obamacare, and to rail against the raising of the federal debt ceiling—the limit on how much the federal government may borrow. Since 1917, when the debt ceiling was created, Congress had voted dozens of times to raise the debt ceiling. Such votes generated little controversy, because they didn't authorize new spending; they merely ensured the federal government would be able to pay for spending Congress had already approved.

In the 2010 midterm elections, the GOP won control of the House with a stunning 63-seat pickup. Republicans gained six seats in the Senate, though Democrats still held the majority in the upper chamber of Congress.

"A HOSTAGE WORTH RANSOMING"

In January 2011, when the 112th Congress convened, 87 of the 242 House Republicans were freshmen. They were a highly conservative lot: more than 40 identified with the Tea Party. By all accounts, the new legislators believed they had a mandate to slash the federal government, and they disdained the notion that they might have to compromise in any way.

The House GOP leadership saw a way to, in the words of congressional scholar Norman Ornstein, "bludgeon President Obama to achieve their goals" of massive spending cuts. Republicans would threaten to vote against the next debt-ceiling increase. If they followed through on that threat, the U.S. government would default on its

President Barack Obama meets with congressional leaders in the White House to discuss ongoing efforts to negotiate an increase in the debt ceiling along with deficit reduction, July 13, 2011. Pictured, from left, are: House Majority Leader Eric Cantor, House Minority Leader Nancy Pelosi, House Speaker John Boehner, Senate Majority Leader Harry Reid, and Senate Minority Leader Mitch McConnell.

debts, which most economists said would produce an economic catastrophe. Obama, Republicans thought, would give in rather than risk that outcome.

However, while the president acknowledged the need for deficit reduction, he insisted that spending cuts be balanced with revenue increases. But almost every Republican in the House had taken the Taxpayer Protection Pledge. Talks between the administration and House leaders foundered over the question of tax hikes.

The federal government was projected to reach its borrowing limit on August 2, 2011. As that date approached, an alarming realization dawned on GOP leaders. Many of the freshmen members they'd fired up for a confrontation were actually willing to allow—and some even seemed to welcome—a U.S. debt default. "Leaders like me," noted Paul Ryan, chairman of the House Budget Committee, "would try to tell them, 'Look, no, really, we think it could be bad.' They'd look at it with suspicion. If there was any semi-credible source saying default wouldn't be so bad, they clung to that."

President Obama and Speaker of the House John Boehner conducted secret talks aimed at concluding a "grand bargain" that would go beyond short-term deficit reduction and put the nation's finances on firm footing over the long haul. Obama offered large cuts to entitlement programs; Boehner, significant revenue increases through reform of the tax code. After weeks of negotiation, it appeared that a deal was imminent. But on July 22, under disputed circumstances, Boehner walked away from the grand bargain.

On August 2, the Budget Control Act cleared Congress and the president signed it into law. The act specified more than $900 billion in spending cuts over a 10-year period, and set up a mechanism for finding an additional $1.5 trillion in cuts, in exchange for an increase in the debt ceiling.

If disaster had been averted at the last minute, the brinkmanship didn't come without cost. For the first time ever, the credit rating of the United States was downgraded. Republicans were criticized for threatening to destroy the economy in pursuit of their agenda. For his part, Mitch McConnell of Kentucky, the Senate minority leader, was remarkably nonchalant. "I think some of our members may have thought the default issue was a hostage you might take a chance at shooting," McConnell said. "Most of us didn't think that. What we did learn is this—it's a hostage that's worth ransoming."

McConnell further suggested that instead of trying to build consensus or compromise with the president and congressional Democrats on budget issues, Republicans would use the same tactic again. "I expect the next president, whoever that is," the minority leader said, "is going to be asking us to raise the debt ceiling again in 2013, so we'll be doing it all over."

DEFEAT AND POSTMORTEM

As the 2012 campaign got under way, Republicans had cause for optimism. A Gallup poll conducted in January found just 18 percent of Americans satisfied with the way things were going in the country. That was the lowest level Gallup had ever recorded in January of a presidential election year. In addition, President Obama's job approval rating consistently stayed below 50 percent.

The 2012 Republican presidential primary field was crowded. But Mitt Romney, the former governor of Massachusetts, ultimately emerged to win the nomination easily. Over the course of his political career, Romney had adopted a variety of moderate or even progressive

Former Massachusetts governor Mitt Romney (right) was the Republican Party's presidential nominee in 2012. Romney chose a conservative congressman from Wisconsin, Paul Ryan, as his running mate, and his campaign was aimed at conservatives and angry Tea Party voters.

positions. For example, he'd promised to be a champion of gay rights during a 1994 Senate campaign. As Massachusetts governor he'd signed a health care reform law that Obamacare would closely resemble.

But during the presidential primary campaign, Romney characterized himself as "severely conservative." He staked out hard-line positions on immigration—suggesting, for example, that if conditions for undocumented immigrants were made sufficiently difficult, those people would "self-deport." Romney also adopted socially conservative positions on various issues affecting women.

On Election Day, Barack Obama secured a second term as president, winning 332 electoral votes to Romney's 206. Obama's popular-vote margin was smaller than in 2008—but at 4 percentage points, it was still comfortable. Democrats also gained two seats in the Senate and eight in the House.

2012 Presidential Election

WA 12
OR 7
ID 6
MT 3
ND 3
MN 10
WI 10
MI 16
NY 29
VT 3
NH
ME 4
MA 11
CT 7
RI 4
WY 3
SD 3
IA 6
IL 20
IN 11
OH 18
PA 20
NJ 14
DE 3
MD 10
DC 3
NV 6
UT 6
CO 9
NE 5
MO 10
KY 8
WV 5
VA 13
NC 15
CA 55
KS 6
OK 7
AR 6
TN 11
SC 9
AZ 11
NM 5
TX 38
MS 6
AL 9
GA 16
LA 8
FL 29
AK 3
HI 4

Mitt Romney (Republican)
60,933,500 popular votes (47.2%)
206 electoral votes

Barack Obama (Democratic)
65,915,796 popular votes (51.1%)
332 electoral votes

In the aftermath of the 2012 election, the Republican National Committee undertook a "postmortem" to identify the reasons for the GOP's failures and to recommend solutions. Among the conclusions of the report issued by the "Growth and Opportunity Project" was that the Republican Party needed to focus on reaching out to women and minorities, large numbers of whom the GOP had alienated with its rhetoric and policies. Mitt Romney had lost the female vote by 11 points, and the Latino vote by a staggering 44 points. His deficits among blacks and Asian Americans were even greater.

The report also noted the party's big problem with younger Americans. Romney had lost voters age 18–29 by 23 percent. A large part of the reason, the report suggested, was that threadbare

Republican policies from the 1980s didn't resonate with young people in a different century—and constantly invoking the name of the 40th president didn't change that fact. "At our core, Republicans have comfortably remained the Party of Reagan without figuring out what comes next," the report said.

> Ronald Reagan is a Republican hero and role model who was first elected 33 years ago—meaning no one under the age of 51 today was old enough to vote for Reagan when he first ran for President. Our Party knows how to appeal to older voters, but we have lost our way with younger ones. We sound increasingly out of touch.

Many political observers publicly wondered whether Reagan could even secure the presidential nomination in the contemporary GOP, given Tea Party conservatives' intense dislike of the kind of compromises he'd deemed necessary in order to govern. "Reagan couldn't have made it," former Senate majority leader and GOP presidential nominee Bob Dole said simply.

RIFTS

Some Republicans heeded the Growth and Opportunity Project's call to mend relations with the Latino community through immigration reform. Fourteen GOP senators joined with all the Senate's Democrats in passing an immigration-reform bill in June 2013. But, in the face of a threatened revolt from the most conservative members of the House Republican conference, Speaker Boehner never brought the immigration bill to a vote.

Boehner would find it increasingly difficult to manage his caucus. Tea Party conservatives demanded repeated, symbolic votes to repeal Obamacare. But they rejected legislation that had formerly been uncontroversial, such as a farm bill and a transportation-funding bill. In October 2013—urged on by Ted Cruz, a freshman Republican senator from Texas—House Republicans tried to use a stopgap-spending bill to defund Obamacare. The result was a 16-day government shutdown and another debt-ceiling crisis.

Polls showed that, by wide margins, more Americans blamed Republicans than Democrats or the president for the political dysfunction. Nonetheless, the GOP won big in the midterm elections one year later. Republicans picked up 13 seats to expand their majority in the House, and they took control of the Senate with a net gain of nine seats.

The GOP's takeover of the Senate elevated Mitch McConnell to the position of majority leader. McConnell promised that, with the Republican Party in control of both chambers of Congress, Americans would see less dysfunction and brinkmanship out of Washington.

But in February 2015, just two months into his tenure as majority leader, McConnell watched helplessly as a shutdown of the Department of Homeland Security loomed. In a DHS funding bill, House Republicans had included provisions to overturn executive actions President Obama had taken on immigration. Those provisions also enjoyed broad support among Republicans in the Senate. But Senate Democrats used a procedural maneuver called the filibuster—which McConnell had deployed relentlessly when the GOP was in the minority in the Senate—to prevent the DHS bill from coming to a vote.

Faced with the prospect of shuttering part of the agency responsible for keeping the United States safe from terrorism, Majority Leader McConnell and Speaker Boehner eventually allowed votes on a DHS funding bill that had been stripped of the immigration amendments. The "clean" bill passed the House only because of Democratic support—a majority of Republicans voted against it. Conservatives were furious at the outcome.

"If we're not going to fight now, when are we going to fight?" fumed Representative Matt Salmon of Arizona, a member of the House GOP's hard-line Freedom Caucus. Countered Representative Charlie Dent, a Republican from Pennsylvania, "It's time for us to move forward and demonstrate our ability to govern to the American people."

Those two reactions to the DHS funding battle reflect a larger struggle going on within today's Republican Party. That struggle, which pits the GOP establishment against Tea Party–influenced insurgents, has little to do with policy. Both sides agree on broad conservative goals such as shrinking government, lowering taxes, and get-

Candidates for the 2016 GOP presidential nomination pose for a photo before a debate at the Reagan Library, September 16, 2015. Donald Trump (eighth from left) was the surprise front-runner for the party's nomination late in 2015, although conservatives like Marco Rubio (fifth from left) and Ted Cruz (sixth from left) were mounting strong challenges.

ting rid of Obamacare. At issue are tactics. Establishment Republicans acknowledge that control of Congress brings a responsibility to govern—and, with a Democrat in the White House, that entails some degree of compromise. Insurgent Republicans continue to equate compromise with capitulation, and they've blasted GOP leaders as sellouts.

As the 2016 presidential race got under way, polling indicated that many rank-and-file Republicans sided with the insurgents. A May 2015 Pew survey found that just 4 in 10 Republicans believed their party's congressional leaders were doing a good job, and three-quarters faulted those leaders for not challenging President Obama enough. By a margin of 73 percent to 21 percent, Republicans in an August 2015 Quinnipiac poll said they wanted an outsider rather than a person with experience in Washington to be their party's presidential nominee.

Whether or not an outsider captured the GOP nomination, the internal struggle for the heart of the Republican Party seemed likely to continue beyond 2016. The divisions within the party run deep.

Chapter Notes

p. 5   "we don't exist . . ." Sophia Tesfaye, "'Cooked as a Party'" Shocker: Republican Chairman Admits 'Terrible Feeling' About GOP's Future," *Salon*, October 16, 2015. http://www.salon.com/2015/10/16/rnc_chair_ admits_the_gop_is_cooked_as_a_party_if_they_lose_the_white_house/

p. 8   "It's an undeniable empirical . . ." Chris Cilizza, "Republicans Have a Major Demographic Problem. And It's Only Going to Get Worse," *Washington Post*, April 22, 2014. https://www.washingtonpost.com/news/ the-fix/wp/2014/04/22/the-republican-demographic-problem-is-just-going-to-keep-getting-worse/

p. 10 "If we continue to come across . . ." Maeve Reston and Seema Mehta, "Republicans Pledge to Change Tone, Not Positions," *Los Angeles Times*, April 12, 2013. http://articles.latimes.com/2013/apr/12/nation/la-na-0413-republicans-20130413

p. 11 "forced to contort themselves . . ." David Frum, "Crashing the Party: Why the GOP Must Modernize to Win," *Foreign Affairs* (September/October 2014). https://www.foreignaffairs.com/articles/united-states/2014-08-18/crashing-party

p. 15 "I think Ronald Reagan . . ." Robert W. Merry, *Where They Stand: The American Presidents in the Eyes of Voters and Historians* (New York: Simon & Schuster, 2012), p. 204.

p. 16 "say that the United States . . ." Ronald Reagan, Republican National Convention acceptance speech (July 17, 1980). Text at Ronald Reagan Presidential Library & Museum, http://www.reagan.utexas.edu/archives/reference/7.17.80.html

p. 16 "at its lowest ebb . . ." Ibid.

p. 17 "unnecessary and excessive . . ." Ronald Reagan, Inaugural Address, January 20, 1981. The American Presidency Project. http://www.presidency.ucsb.edu/ws/?pid = 43130

p. 17 "In this present crisis . . ." Ibid.

p. 18 "I hope you're a Republican," Richard Reeves, *President Reagan: The Triumph of Imagination* (New York: Simon & Schuster, 2005), p. 38.

p. 19 "Ronald Reagan was never afraid . . ." Brian Montopoli, "Ronald Reagan Myth Doesn't Square with Reality," CBS News, February 4, 2011. http://www.cbsnews.com/news/ronald-reagan-myth-doesnt-square-with-reality/

p. 19   "oppose and vote against . . ." Americans for Tax Reform website. http://www.atr.org/about

p. 19   "I don't want to abolish . . ." Monika Bauerlein and Clara Jeffery, "The Job Killers," *Mother Jones* (November/December 2011). http://www.motherjones.com/politics/2011/10/republicans-job-creation-kill

p. 20   "would never again mount . . ." Lou Cannon, *President Reagan: The Role of a Lifetime* (New York: PublicAffairs, 2000), p. 214.

p. 20   "was reduced to tinkering . . ." Ibid.

p. 22   "momentous achievement," Earl Black and Merle Black, *The Rise of Southern Republicans* (Cambridge, MA: Harvard University Press, 2009), p. 205.

p. 22   "By transforming the region's . . ." Ibid.

p. 23   "It was a matter . . ." Tom Bowman, "Reagan Guided Huge Buildup in Arms Race," *Baltimore Sun*, June 8, 2004. http://www.baltimoresun.com/news/bal-te.pentagon08jun08-story.html

p. 23   "I began to realize . . ." David E. Hoffman, "In 1983 'War Scare,' Soviet Leadership Feared Nuclear Surprise Attack by U.S.," *Washington Post*, October 24, 2015. https://www.washingtonpost.com/world/national-security/in-1983-war-scare-soviet-leadership-feared-nuclear-surprise-attack-by-us/2015/10/24/15a289b4-7904-11e5-a958-d889faf561dc_story.html

p. 25   "Read my lips . . ." George Bush, Address Accepting the Presidential Nomination at the Republican National Convention in New Orleans, August 18, 1988. American Presidency Project. http://www.presidency.ucsb.edu/ws/?pid = 25955

p. 25   "America is a rising nation," Ibid.

p. 25   "want power in the hands . . ." Ibid.

p. 28   "There is not a program . . ." William J. Clinton, Address Accepting the Presidential Nomination at the Democratic National Convention in New York, July 16, 1992. The American Presidency Project. http://www.presidency.ucsb.edu/ws/?pid = 25958

p. 28   "end welfare as we . . ." Ibid.

p. 29   "We are buying . . ." Bob Herbert, "In America; The Doom Mongers," *New York Times*, November 6, 1994. http://www.nytimes.com/1994/11/06/opinion/in-america-the-doom-mongers.html

p. 29   "The tax increase will kill jobs . . ." Mark Shields, "A Tough One for Clinton," *Washington Post*, August 12, 2000. https://www.washingtonpost.com/archive/opinions/2000/08/12/a-tough-one-for-clinton/2dbafdc3-142e-4557-abe1-b6a563aa6bc6/

p. 30   "restore fiscal responsibility . . ." "The Republican 'Contract with America.'" Prentice Hall Documents Library.

http://wps.prenhall.com/wps/media/objects/434/445252/DocumentsLibrary/docs/contract.htm

p. 30   "to replace career politicians . . ." Ibid.

p. 31   "do my dead level best," Adam Clymer, "The 1994 Elections: Congress the Overview; G.O.P. Celebrates Its Sweep to Power; Clinton Vows to Find Common Ground," *New York Times*, November 10, 1994. http://www.nytimes.com/1994/11/10/us/1994-elections-congress-overview-gop-celebrates-its-sweep-power-clinton-vows.html?pagewanted = all

p. 31   "You just wonder . . ." "Gingrich Comment on Shutdown Labeled 'Bizarre' by White House," CNN, November 16, 1995. http://www.cnn.com/US/9511/debt_limit/11-16/budget_gingrich/

p. 32   "The era of big Government . . ." William J. Clinton, Address Before a Joint Session of Congress on the State of the Union, January 23, 1996. The American Presidency Project. http://www.presidency.ucsb.edu/ws/?pid = 53091

p. 32   "we cannot go back . . ." Ibid.

p. 34   "The GOP is standing in quicksand," Paul West, "Aftermath of Impeachment: Campaign 2000," *Baltimore Sun*, February 14, 1999. http://articles.baltimore-sun.com/1999-02-14/news/9902160276_1_clinton-scandal-impeachment-bill-clinton

p. 35   "People think oftentimes . . ." E. J. Dionne, *Stand Up Fight Back: Republican Toughs, Democratic Wimps, and the Politics of Revenge* (New York, Simon & Schuster, 2004), p. 25.

p. 37   "giving the most . . ." Richard W. Stevenson, "Bush Signs Tax Cut Bill, Dismissing All Criticism," *New York Times*, May 29, 2003. http://www.nytimes.com/2003/05/29/us/bush-signs-tax-cut-bill-dismissing-all-criticism.html

p. 38   "By giving individuals more money . . ." Jarrett Murphy, "Bush Signs Tax Cuts into Law," CBS News, May 21, 2003. http://www.cbsnews.com/news/bush-signs-tax-cuts-into-law/

p. 38   "the largest expansion of the welfare state . . ." Bruce Bartlett, "Medicare Part D: Republican Budget-Busting," *New York Times*, November 19, 2013. http://economix.blogs.nytimes.com/2013/11/19/medicare-part-d-republican-budget-busting/

p. 38   "to use all necessary . . ." Text of Authorization for Use of Military Force (Sept. 18, 2001). https://www.govtrack.us/congress/bills/107/sjres23/text

p. 39   "our war on terror . . ." "Text: President Bush Addresses the Nation," *Washington Post*, September 20, 2001. http://www.washingtonpost.com/wp-srv/nation/specials/attacked/transcripts/bushaddress_092001.html

p. 39   "possesses and produces . . ." "Bush: Don't Wait for Mushroom Cloud," CNN,

October 8, 2002.
http://edition.cnn.com/2002/ALLPOLITICS/10/07/bush.transcript/

p. 40   "I really do believe . . ." George Packer, *The Assassins' Gate: America in Iraq* (New York: Farrar, Straus and Giroux, 2005), p. 97.

p. 41   "Major combat operations . . ." Seth Cline, "The Other Symbol of George W. Bush's Legacy," *U.S. News & World Report*, May 1, 2013.
http://www.usnews.com/news/blogs/press-past/2013/05/01/the-other-symbol-of-george-w-bushs-legacy

p. 44   "Everyone's got to stick together," Robert Draper, *Do Not Ask What Good We Do: Inside the U.S. House of Representatives* (New York: Free Press, 2012), xvii.

p. 44   "If you act like you're . . ." Ibid., xviii.

p. 46   "bludgeon President Obama . . ." Jason M. Breslow, "The GOP Freshmen of 2010: 'Spear Carriers' with a Mission," *PBS Frontline*, February 12, 2013.
http://www.pbs.org/wgbh/frontline/article/the-gop-freshmen-of-2010-spear-carriers-with-a-mission/

p. 47   "Leaders like me . . ." Brady Dennis et al., "Origins of the Debt Showdown," *Washington Post*, August 6, 2011.
https://www.washingtonpost.com/business/economy/origins-of-the-debt-showdown/2011/08/03/gIQA9uqIzI_story.html

p. 48   "I think some of our members . . ." Thomas E. Mann and Norman J. Ornstein, *It's Even Worse Than It Looks: How the American Constitutional System Collided with the New Politics of Extremism* (New York: Basic Books, 2102), p. 25.

p. 48   "I expect the next president . . ." Ibid., pp. 25–26.

p. 51   "At our core . . ." Republican National Committee, "Growth & Opportunity Project" (March 18, 2013), p. 5.

p. 51   "Reagan couldn't have made it," Mark Sappenfield, "Bob Dole Says Reagan Couldn't Make It in Today's GOP. Is He Right?" *Christian Science Monitor*, May 26, 2013. http://www.csmonitor.com/USA/Politics/DC-Decoder/2013/0526/Bob-Dole-says-Reagan-couldn-t-make-it-in-today-s-GOP.-Is-he-right

p. 52   "If we're not going to fight . . ." Beau Yarbrough, et al., "Congress Sends Homeland Security Bill to Obama Without Immigration Conditions," *Los Angeles Daily News*, March 3, 2015. http://www.dailynews.com/government-and-politics/20150303/congress-sends-homeland-security-bill-to-obama-without-immigration-conditions

p. 52   "It's time for us . . ." Susan Davis and Erin Kelly, "House Funds Homeland Security Without Immigration Riders," *USA Today*, March 3, 2015.
http://www.usatoday.com/story/news/politics/2015/03/03/house-homeland-security-funding-vote/24308531/

Glossary

activist—a person who campaigns for political or social causes.

affiliation—connection with a group or organization, such as a political party.

brinkmanship—the practice of pushing a dangerous situation to the limit of safety, in order to obtain concessions from an adversary.

budget deficit—a situation in which a government's spending exceeds its revenue.

budget surplus—a situation in which a government's revenue exceeds its spending.

bureaucracy—a large group of people who are involved in running a government but who are not elected.

census—an official count of a nation's population.

coalition—a temporary alliance of individuals, parties, or states.

communism—a political and economic system that calls for the elimination of private property, promotes the common ownership of goods, and usually insists that the Communist Party has sole authority to govern.

constituency—a group of people who support or are likely to support a political party or candidate.

demographics—the characteristics (such as age, sex, race or ethnicity, and income) of a specific group of people; a group of people that has a particular set of characteristics.

electorate—all the people who are entitled to vote, or who actually vote, in an election.

ideology—a set of ideas or beliefs of a political party or other group.

incumbent—someone who holds a political office and is campaigning for reelection.

national budget—a document specifying the amount of money the federal government expects to raise in taxes or acquire through loans and the amount of money the government plans to spend on its programs during the course of a year.

national debt—the amount of money the federal government owes.

national security—the concept that the federal government should defend a country against threats from within and from outside its borders.

New Deal—a series of domestic programs enacted in the United States between 1933 and 1938.

primary election—an election to determine a political party's nominee for the presidency or other office.

recession—a period of temporary economic decline.

rhetoric—a type or mode of language or speech, used typically for the purpose of argument or persuasion.

Further Reading

Cannon, Lou. *President Reagan: The Role of a Lifetime*. New York: PublicAffairs, 2000.

Critchlow, Donald T. *The Conservative Ascendancy: How the GOP Right Made Political History*. Cambridge, MA: Harvard University Press, 2007.

Draper, Robert. *Do Not Ask What Good We Do: Inside the U.S. House of Representatives*. New York: Free Press, 2012.

Meacham, Jon. *Destiny and Power: The American Odyssey of George Herbert Walker Bush*. New York: Random House, 2015.

Richardson, Heather Cox. *To Make Men Free: A History of the Republican Party*. New York: Basic Books, 2014.

Skocpol, Theda, and Vanessa Williamson. *The Tea Party and the Remaking of Republican Conservatism*. New York: Oxford University Press, 2012.

Internet Resources

https://www.gop.com
> Home page of the Republican National Committee.

http://rsc.flores.house.gov/
> The website of the Republican Study Committee, a caucus of conservative Republicans in the House of Representatives, offers news, analysis of legislation, and more.

http://www.republican.senate.gov/public/
> Press releases, policy papers, news, videos, and more from the Senate Republican conference.

http://www.rollcall.com
> The online version of *Roll Call*, a Washington, D.C.–based newspaper focusing on politics and policy.

http://www.archives.gov/federal-register/electoral-college
> This website managed by the National Archives provides information about the Electoral College and includes results of past presidential elections.

Index

African Americans, 9, 10, 22, 28, 50
al-Qaeda, 38–39, 41
American Recovery and Reinvestment Act (ARRA), 44
American Values Survey, 11–12
America's New Beginning report, 17

Balanced Budget Act of 1997, 33
Barbour, Haley, 11
Bartlett, Bruce, 38
bin Laden, Osama, 39
Black, Earl, 22
Black, Merle, 22
Boehner, John, 47–48, 51, 52
Brinkley, Douglas, 19
Budget Control Act, 48
budget deficits, federal, 17, 18, 20, 27, 29
budget surpluses, federal, 29, 33, 38
Bush, George H. W., 25–27, 28–29, 35
Bush, George W., 35–36, 37–39, 42, 43
  and the Iraq War, 39–42

Campbell, Ben Nighthorse, 34
Cannon, Lou, 20
Cantor, Eric, 46, *47*
Carter, Jimmy, 16, 20, 21
Cheney, Dick, 40
Clinton, Bill, 27–33

and impeachment, 33–34
Cold War, 22–24
Contract with America, 30
  See also Republican Revolution
Cruz, Ted, 51, *53*

debt ceiling, federal, 46–48, 51
Democratic Party, 8, 12, 13, 14
  and demographics, 6, 9–11
Dent, Charlie, 52
Dole, Bob, *32*, 33, 51
Draper, Robert, 44
Dukakis, Michael, 25–26
DW-NOMINATE, 6–7

Economic Growth and Tax Relief Reconciliation Act (EGTRRA), 37
Economic Recovery Tax Act (ERTA), 18
economy, 16, 25, 27, 43
  and legislation, 18–19, 29, 32–33, 37–38, 44, 48
  and supply-side economics, 17–18, 29
  See also tax
elections
  midterm, 20, 26, 29–30, 34, 40, 42, 46, 52
  presidential, 5–6, 8, 16, 21, 22, 26, 28–29, 33, 35–37, 42, 43–44, 48–50, 53

Frist, Bill, 38

Frum, David, 11

Gerson, David, 35
Gingrich, Newt, 29, 30–32, 34
Gorbachev, Mikhail, 23–24
Gore, Al, *31*, 35–36
government
  role of the, 11–12, 15, 17, 19–20, 32, 44–45
Gramm, Phil, 29
Grand Old Party (GOP). *See* Republican Party
"Great Communicator." *See* Reagan, Ronald
Gulf War, *26*, 27, 39
gun rights, **5**, 13, 14

health care, **5**, 13, 30, 33, 45–46
Hispanic demographic. *See* Latinos
House of Representatives, 34
  Democratic majorities in the, 18, 20, 22, 26, 29, 30, 42, 43–44, 46
  Republican majorities in the, 5, 30–31, 36–37, 40, 52
Hussein, Saddam, 39, 40, 41

immigration, 13, 49, 51, 52
Iraq War, 39–43

Jeffords, Jim, 37
Jobs and Growth Tax Relief Reconciliation Act

Numbers in ***bold italic*** refer to captions.

62

About the Author

John Ziff is a write and editor. He lives near Philadelphia. His books for young adults include *The Bombing of Hiroshima* (Chelsea House, 2002), *The Causes of World War I* (OTTN Publishing, 2005), *Gun Laws* (Eldorado Ink, 2014), *The Korean War* (Mason Crest, 2015) and *Northeast: New Jersey, New York, Pennsylvania* (Mason Crest, 2015).